Made in United States
North Haven, CT
06 March 2023

33667829R00057